# don't
## feed the
# seagulls

*a book of
inspirational
poetry*

# byron von rosenberg

PRESS

ACW Press
Eugene, Oregon 97405

Cover Design by Alpha Advertising
Interior design by Pine Hill Graphics

Packaged by ACW Press
85334 Lorane Hwy
Eugene, Oregon 97405
www.acwpress.com
The views expressed or implied in this work do not necessarily reflect those of ACW Press. Ultimate design, content, and editorial accuracy of this work is the responsibility of the author(s).

Publisher's Cataloging-in-Publication Data
*(Provided by Cassidy Cataloguing Services, Inc.)*

von Rosenberg, Byron.

    Don't feed the seagulls / Byron von Rosenberg. --1st ed. --
Eugene, OR : ACW Press, 2003.

    p. ; cm.

    ISBN: 1-932124-13-6

    1. Poetry. I. Title

PS3618.O74 A17 2003
811.6--dc21                0306

**Printed in the United States of America.**

# Dedication

*D*on't *Feed the Seagulls* is dedicated to my father. Dr. Dale Ursini von Rosenberg was an exceptionally intelligent man who saw the beauty and nature of God in many things: the laws of mathematics that he knew and loved so well, baseball, music, a good book, God's great out-of-doors, and especially friends and family. He gave expression to his knowledge through the love he poured out to those around him. And he was greatly blessed to spend the last forty-nine years of his life as Marjorie's husband.

My father battled ALS the last two and a half years of his life. He fought valiantly and used all his strength, his will, and his faith to sustain himself. His last battle was to live to see his whole family gathered about him one last time. As he counted the days, hours, and minutes until everyone arrived, he seemed like the marathon runner entering the stadium for the final lap. With no energy left, he looked within and found a deep resolve; he looked about and found the support of his family and many friends, and he looked above and found the greatest strength of all. Then, like that tired marathon runner, he willed himself forward, across the finish line. We lifted him on our shoulders for a victory lap, and then God lifted him higher to glory in heaven.

I watched my father's struggle and asked God to help me understand. He gave me this poem to write. It is a prayer and a conversation between God, a father, and a son.

## Look at My Hands

Look at my hands, now crippled and old,
Once so strong, now what can they hold?
THEY HOLD THE LOVE I GAVE TO YOU,
YOU PASSED IT ON, YET IT STAYED AND GREW.

I felt it, Dad, when you held me high,
   I laughed and sang and touched the sky.
I felt God's love when you passed it through
   And now I'm here to bring it back to you.

Look at my feet, I can barely stand,
   They climbed tall mountains and crossed the land!
THEY CARRY THE MESSAGE OF JESUS' LOVE
   HIGHER THAN MOUNTAINTOPS
      TO HEAVEN ABOVE.
I followed you, Dad, to that highest peak
   And I followed you, Dad, our Savior to seek.
Your feet led me to Him when I was a boy,
   With Him in our hearts, each day's filled with joy.

It's so hard to breathe, the air is so thin,
   I want to shout and sing praises again.
I STILL HEAR THE SONGS AND THE PRAISES YOU LIFT,
   COME SING THEM IN HEAVEN
      WHERE NEW LIFE IS YOUR GIFT!
You taught me to sing, Dad, with you I give praise
   And I thank God today I was your son to raise.
All of your family and your many friends too,
   Each of us, all of us, see Jesus in you.

He's my Daddy, Lord, I can't say good-bye,
   Whatever you do, please don't let him die!
THE LOVE THAT I GAVE HIM HE PASSED ON TO YOU,
   NOW PASS IT TO OTHERS AND WATCH IT RENEW.
Don't fret over me, son, I've been born again,
   I'm living in heaven and free from all sin.
My hands are strong, my feet can run,
   Hear me shout, "Hallelujah, the Victory's won!"

I hope that you will enjoy reading this book and feel the Holy Spirit's presence in the poems. And perhaps you will find a little of my father there as well. May God bless you and your family this day and always,

Yours in Christ,

Byron von Rosenberg
February 15, 2003
House Springs, Missouri

# Acknowledgments

*T*his literary journey began with the poem I received and wrote for my father. At that time I prayed for the Holy Spirit to continue to bless me in this way. *Don't Feed the Seagulls* is the first result. Each poem has been a unique gift, and I hope that you find a special message in one or more of them. Along with the Holy Spirit there are many people without whom the completion of this book would not have been possible.

I have been blessed with a loving and supportive wife and wonderful children. Sharon has been encouraging me to write since hearing me tell bedtime stories to Ryan and Erin when they were little. I could not have written this book without her or them.

I also have had most wonderful support from all my family. A special thanks goes to my brother Gene. I've included a new poem dedicated to him; it's called "The Toy Bugle" and I believe you'll enjoy it. My mother, Marjorie, has been wonderful as well, often providing insight and wisdom into how a story or poem can be made better. Alyene Pierot, my mother-in-law, has been a great source of Christian wisdom and strength. My sister Carol and her husband, Brad, my brother Clyde, and their families have also encouraged and supported me Also, my father's brothers Hermann and Charles, and their wives, Annelle and Caroline, have been of great help. I thank them all.

My friend Joe Galbraith from Corpus Christi, Texas always makes me feel good with his kind remarks. I'd also like to thank my friends in Troop 387 at St. John's United Church of Christ, Manchester, Missouri, for allowing me to "field test" these poems. It's a really good feeling when teenage boys appreciate your poetry. Actually, it's nice when anyone does! That includes the fine residents and staff of the Meramec Bluffs, Laclede Groves, Nazareth, and Marymount Retirement communities and the members of the St. Louis West Optimists' Club, each of whom allowed me to read my poems to them based only on our initial conversations.

I'd also like to thank my friends in the Boy Scout organization for their heartfelt condolences and concern upon the death of my father. While this book is in no way associated with or endorsed by the Boy Scouts of America, some of the poems were inspired by my Scouting experiences.

Special acknowledgment goes to Fred and Lenora Richter, Meshack Ilobi and Tina Wong, our very special friends whose actions have given us inspiration.

And we send our special thanks to the Vicky Appel ALS Clinic in Houston, Texas and to Lone Star Hospice for their patience, understanding and care for my father and family.

Finally and most importantly, thank You, Jesus, for Your incredible gift of eternal life in heaven! May this book help spread Your Word.

Byron von Rosenberg
February 10, 2003
House Springs, Missouri

# Contents

Note: A Seagull (  ) at the
end of a page indicates that
the same poem continues on
the next page.

# Foreword

Since I have no way of knowing what decision or experience prompted you to pick up this book or what you expect or hope to find in its poems, let me tell you my personal experience. The first time I knew that my nephew had tried his hand at poetry was at "A Service of Witness to the Resurrection" in Georgetown, Texas, last July for my brother, Dale. Byron agreed to speak for the family about his father and our many memories of him. He concluded with a poem he had written the week before. It is the poem "Look at My Hands" included with the Dedication of this volume.

We understood that there were already other poems he had written and that we should expect more to come. Over the next several months, at odd moments, we would hear from Byron by telephone. Each time he would read to us one or more new poems often relating the experience that had led to its writing. His excitement was obvious, and the fascinating variety of ideas which caught his attention on ordinary days is reflected in the poems gathered here.

Stroll now through the pages of this book, stopping at the titles which catch your attention. Expect to be amused by many. But do not be surprised if your eyes moisten now and then when deep emotive chords are struck. Among them you will find many which address the spirit within us. And there are others, which like fables, begin by pointing to behavior patterns of some of our animal friends and end up exposing the foibles of human life on this planet.

If it helps, read the poems out loud to yourself or better yet to friends and family. These poems may help you look down again to the tiny creatures at your feet, around to the broader scope of modern life with all its complexities, and up to the splendors of heaven above with God's love and grace never far behind the scenes.

Rev. Charles E. von Rosenberg
February 10, 2003
Rock Hill, South Carolina

## Chapter One

# Don't Feed
# the Seagulls

### Don't Feed the Seagulls

"Daddy, you can't feed the seagulls here," said my son,
    "It says so on that sign.
If you do you'll have to pay
    'Cause there's a hundred dollar fine."
But the seagulls must not have read those words
    And hungry they must be
For them to take a cracker
    From a lawbreaker like me.
As I hold each cracker high
    The seagulls gather to be fed
Like famished spirits waiting
    For what nourishes much more than bread.
"Do not feed the seagulls!"
    In China or Bangladesh,
For we're afraid what will happen here
    If they taste what's good and fresh.
But yes, I WILL feed the seagulls
    On this or any beach
And I will spread the Gospel
    Until the whole wide world I reach.

## Forget Your Umbrella

I went out without my umbrella today
    And left my raincoat in the hall,
Not the smartest thing to do
    On a dark day in the fall.
The clouds soon opened and rain poured down,
    I was drenched from head to toe,
But instead of being angry
    I remembered a child of long ago:
The child who ran out when it rained
    And rode bikes in flooded streets,
The one who built a giant pond
    And sailed those mighty fleets.
I'm the one who laughed at clouds,
    "Rain more on me!" I cried;
I had to dry out on the porch
    Before Mom let me inside.
God's gifts come pouring down like rain,
    So many I once knew,
But until today I was dry,
    Untouched even by the dew.
But now I'm drenched again
    As the waters of heaven pour
And though I'm soaking to the skin
    I want it to rain some more.

---

## Don't Pick It Up, It's Dirty

"Don't pick that up, it's dirty,
    Just leave it on the ground;
You don't need a coin like that,
    It's not good to have around."

These words are right, I know they are,
    For we must hang on to what's good,
But I wonder what that coin would say
    If talk to me it could.
Would it tell me that it bought some soup
    For a dying man to eat?
And did it buy a child's ice cream cone
    Before it landed on the street?
If I scraped off all that dirt
    Underneath would I find gold?
And if I got to know you well,
    Could I ever again act so cold?
For the world is good at hiding us
    And coating us with fear;
I've looked long and hard for Jesus
    And there He was, right here.

---

## *Fall on Me*

The snowfall was different this time,
    Even prettier and a brighter, cleaner white;
It settled quietly over everything
    As it fell throughout the night.
The snowplows didn't roll at all;
    Everyone stayed at home all through the day
But the snow didn't freeze their fingers
    When the children went out to play.
When they rolled it up to make a snowman,
    The grass beneath had turned to green;
The snow melted in the streets that day
    But the pavement was sparkling clean.
The trash had strangely disappeared,
    Not a bit was ever found.

Scientists sampled the frozen soil
    And said you could eat off of the ground.
A snowball hit a deaf girl's ear,
    Now she hears clear as a bell;
A sickly boy ate some of it
    And instantly got well.
A children's story or a fairy tale?
    Oh no, this story is quite true,
For Jesus sent the snow that day
    To fall on me and you.

## A Moment Away

I waded in waist-deep waters
    As the afternoon sun danced on the ocean.
In the distance sailboats drifted by;
    Even the seagulls flew in slow motion.
The warm touch of the waves melted my cares
    And the cool breeze caressed my face.
It seemed as though the clocks had stopped
    And I was alone in time and space.
Suddenly the water moved!
    A dark, gray form surged from the sand below—
My heart leapt with it—
    Water too deep! Feet too slow!

Instantly a life can change
    Without warning or compassion or alarm.
Things that we've worked for, people we love
    Can suffer irreparable harm
Or even be lost. And we, too, suffer the cost
    As we try to understand and adjust,

So we cry out in vain,
    "Lord how can we ever again trust?
So much have we lost
    And the pain is so great.
Lord where's your plan now,
    Is it just up to fate?"

The manta ray surfaced in front of me
    Then submerged again out of sight.
I was the only one who saw it
    And no one else shared my fright.
Danger lurks always, only a moment away.
    Fight it! Defeat it! Lift your hands and pray!

---

## The Storm

We saw the dark clouds quickly gather
    And felt the cold wind blow;
The lightning flashed and shattered
    The trees and rocks below.
We ran down the rocky mountain
    Seeking cover in this place,
To stand alone before that storm
    Was a danger we'd dare not face.
We kept running and sliding down
    To get to lower ground;
We took the trail we thought was safe
    Then our leader stopped and frowned.
"This trail has led to the top again,"
    His voice was fraught with fear;
We felt the rain begin to fall
    For the storm was now right here.

When the storms of life assail you
    And in your own wisdom you do trust,
Does the trail you choose lead back to the storm
    And into the wind's strong gust?
When you're powerless against the storm
    And you have no place to hide,
That's the time to kneel in prayer,
    Ask Jesus to be your guide.

As we stood there so small and weak
    The clouds parted to blue;
God had stopped the storm for us
    And He'll do the same for you.

             For Charlie

## *The Dolphin*

Hey there, Dolphin, out in the sea,
    What's it like to be so free?
You've no job to make you go away
    So with your family you just stay.
The Lord provides fish for every meal,
    I wish I had such a deal!
For man his daily bread must earn,
    Send our children to school to learn
And then work hard for many years
    And faced with sorrow blink back the tears.
We face the world when we'd rather hide
    So for our families we can provide.
But I see you swimming with your kin,
    No car to drive, you just flip your fin.
No bills to pay or keys to lose,
    Do you do whatever you choose?

It seems so different here on land
    Though God can count each grain of sand.
Each bird and fish and man He knows
    And until He wills it no wind blows.
But we worry so about everything,
    Trying to avoid life's cruel sting;
Should we be more like you,
    Swimming, gliding our whole life through?
Jesus told us be anxious not,
    How is it we so soon forgot?
Perhaps He sent you here today
    To dance for me in foam and spray
To remind me He knows my every need
    And that my soul He's already freed.

---

## Mr. Crow

Don't look so cross at me, Mr. Crow,
    Yes, I disturbed your lunch, I know,
But you spread your wings and off you flew;
    That's a power no man ever knew.
Yes, I see you staring from that tree
    But inside you're laughing hard at me,
"Poor little man, he can't fly,
    He'll never get very high."
But listen here my feathered friend,
    If in truth God did not intend
For man to rise from the ground below
    Then why'd he give me all this to know?
For I can watch and I can learn
    And with my heart and mind I yearn

To rise above this worldly place
   And God's glory to embrace,
For God has set my spirit free
   And I'll fly with you, wait and see.

---

## *Wet Paint*

I took my four-year-old daughter
   To our church's playground to use the swings
But they were painting all the seats
   And the other wooden things.
A big sign said "The paint is wet!"
   So I knew we must not touch
But my daughter couldn't read it yet
   And the temptation grew too much.
Before I could move to stop her
   She was sitting on the seat
And when she ran upon the asphalt
   She marked it with painted feet.
Paint was everywhere about,
   On clothes, on her, on me.
Oh, we had been to church that day,
   A fact that all could see.
I wonder if without the paint on us
   Our choice would be known or seen;
It's hard to tell who's been to church
   Even if your eyesight's keen.
Perhaps if we wore our faith outside
   Like my daughter wore the paint
They'd see the love of Christ on us
   And the footprints of a saint.

—⸙—

## The Katydid

Twenty-six miles across that lake!
How much more can that little bug take?
To that mirror stuck like glue,
Is there a message here for you?
What to do when the strong winds blow,
Do you hang on tight or just let go?
Can you make it though the journey's long,
Fight for what's right and against what is wrong?
And can you hold out against a foolish dare?
Look deep inside; the answer is there.
Inside that bug God put a will to live,
So how much more to you did He give?
So stick to your faith whatever price you must pay
And hang on to Jesus, let nothing pull you away.

—⸙—

## Standing Alone

There on the top of the hill
Is a tree that stands alone;
Where all other trees have died
This one has thrived and grown.
How did a single tree survive
On a hill so tall and steep?
This tree stood fast through all the storms
Because its roots run very deep.

Man is like lilies in the field
With no roots to hold to soil;

The wind can blow him all about
    And his life is filled with toil.
Yet there are things that give a man
    Roots planted deeply in the ground;
The Word of God will keep him safe
    When those final trumpets sound.

It still stands alone atop the hill
    Though others are felled and broken
And he can stand amidst the storm
    For Jesus' name he's spoken.
It may stand for a thousand years,
    Long even for a tree;
But with Jesus in his heart
    He'll live for eternity.

## Chapter Two

---

# America Is

### America Is

America is baseball on a hot summer's day,
　It's fireworks at the grandstand
　　When the band begins to play,
Family picnics in the park, taking children to the zoo,
　The freedom to do the work you love
　　And to love the work you do.
Americans are people who hold their families dear
　And all of us will rally round
　　When our neighbor's call we hear.
America blessed with bounty, America the land we love,
　Our liberty a legacy from the hand of God above.

America is patriots' dreams as they cross the Delaware,
　It's engineers and astronauts as into space we dare.
It's soldiers who defend our homes here or across the sea,
　Citizens who cast their votes
　　So thoughts and words stay free.
Americans are people who hold their heroes high,
　We're heroes one and all
　　When we answer freedom's holy cry.
America home to heroes, America the land we love,
　Our liberty a legacy from the hand of God above.

America is ideas free from fear and doubt,
　Ideas grown inside our minds for voices to let out.

So let me hear you speak that mind even if we don't agree;
    We're family through our freedom
        And that kinship is the key.
Americans are people whose thoughts are free to roam,
    Thoughts to take us to the stars
        And bring us safe back home.
America, ideas' island, America the land we love,
    Our liberty a legacy from the hand of God above.

America is God's blessed land, a people to be born,
    Born in freedom to celebrate and blow the victory horn.
America, God's gift to us, indeed to all the earth,
    For Americans know freedom
        And they know what freedom's worth.
Americans are people who on Almighty God depend,
    Because we live in Him our land He will defend.
America full of faith, America the land we love,
    Our liberty a legacy from the hand of God above.

---

## Our Nation His Creation

As God set forth a new nation
    We set out now as His creation,
For no nation has He blessed like ours
    From fertile fields to glistening towers.
Therefore let us kneel to pray
    For God's hand in our lives today;
Over mountains tall and rivers grand,
    God bless this people and God bless this land!

This gift of bounty has been ours
    And preserved us against all earthly powers;

Our nation is now the strongest yet
    But our Protector we must not forget.
May He save us now from deceitful hearts
    For all our blessings He imparts;
Grantor of victories in an unbroken strand,
    God bless this people and God bless this land!

We lift our eyes toward heavenly air
    And ask You grant our humble prayer:
Forgive us Lord for our national pride;
    We need Your redeeming grace inside.
Please see us through these difficult days,
    For clemency we offer praise,
And on Your side we'll make our stand;
    God bless this nation and God bless this land!

Inspired by a prayer by Abraham Lincoln found in *The Wit and Wisdom of Abraham Lincoln*, Alex Ayers, ed., (Penguin Books, 375 Hudson Street, New York, NY 10014), 1992.

## *Fourth of July*

Two centuries have long since passed
    Since that fateful July four;
Today we once more celebrate
    Though we know not what's in store.
Yet our fathers also did not know
    Where their trail would lead
But they fought and lived and died
    And for that we all are freed.
Years of strife and toil
    Led to better days;
People came together
    To sing and offer praise.

Happy days of summer seen
    In children long grown old,
In photographs they carry flags
    Lifted high to wave and hold.
We offer thanks today
    For the children they were then
And that when they grew up
    They fought so hard to win.
Today the torch has passed to us,
    We also hold it high;
We will carry on in spite of all
    The dangers that grow nigh.
Our children wave that flag today
    And smile and cheer and shout;
With picnics, bands, and fireworks
    In them we'll leave no doubt
That America, the land we love
    Is the greatest land of all
And in its greatest hour of need
    Our children will stand tall!

---

## Nine-One-One

Nine-one-one, Nine-one-one,
Glistening towers in the sun,
Nine-one-one, Nine-one-one,
The Pentagon in Washington,
Nine-one-one, Nine-one-one.

Evil assassins armed with knives,
A plane into a building dives,
Innocent victims who lost their lives,
But America awakened—still survives!

Nine-one-one, Nine-one-one,
A plane into a field that spun,
Nine-one-one, Nine-one-one,
America recovering from the stun,
Nine-one-one, Nine-one-one.

Help victims first, that's what to do,
Hug and cry, but work on through.
We'll clean it up and rebuild it too,
Now we're coming after you!

Nine-one-one, Nine-one-one,
America under the gun,
Nine-one-one, Nine-one-one,
Now we'll put evil on the run,
Nine-one-one, Nine-one-one.

There is no place on earth to hide,
Americans have God's strength inside,
With American work and American pride
We'll avenge our brothers and sisters who died!

Nine-one-one, Nine-one-one,
We'll lift the load though it weigh many a ton,
Nine-one-one, Nine-one-one,
Together we'll see this evil undone,
Nine-one-one, Nine-one-one.

If you thought we'd quit you lost that bet,
Such evil and cowardice we'll never forget!
Our hearts are steeled and our minds are set,
We promise we'll repay this debt—
And rid the world of your evil yet!

Nine-one-one, Nine-one-one,
We won't quit 'til the job is done,
Nine-one-one, Nine-one-one,
Until the final victory's won!
Nine-one-one, Nine-one-one.

America the cradle of liberty,
A shining beacon for all to see,
We'll be the best that we can be,
America first and always free!

Nine-one-one, Nine-one-one,
Join in solemn contemplation,
Nine-one-one, Nine-one-one,
United now, a single nation,
Nine-one-one, Nine-one-one.

Glistening towers in the sun,
The Pentagon in Washington,
We won't quit 'til the job is done,
Until the final victory's won!
Nine-one-one, Nine-one-one...

---

## *September 11, 2002*

The day is much like a year ago
    With blue skies and gentle breeze;
We're each praying, in our own quiet way
    Not again, Lord. Not ever. Please.
The calm and quiet has returned
    And to work and school we go
But there is still a job to do
    A big one, and we all know.
Can we band together again
    Like we did in that first hour
And do we still rely on God
    For His almighty power?
The weather reassures us now,
    It says that nothing's changed,

But we know better than to think that,
    Whole lives are rearranged.
We'll move forward proud and tall
    And knowing that all is dust,
But sure in the victory the day will bring
    For in God we've placed our trust.

---

## *Do Not Open Until 2276*

Fifty-three weeks have passed
    Since that fateful day last year
When we found a different world,
    One we learned to fear.
But you are distant, far away,
    And we don't know what or how you think;
Have we and our children's children
    Brought the world back from the brink?
Do Israelis and Palestinians still fight?
    Does Iraq still pose a threat?
How many billion people live today?
    Has Jesus come back yet?
Do you even remember
    The events of September last
Or is that date just a little part
    Of your forgotten past?
We were children who watched one day
    When our president died on TV;
We saw an iron wall come down
    When people rose up to be free.
Most of us lived quiet lives
    Raising families and paying bills;
We put our faith in God above
    Who our every need fulfills.

Were we able to pass to you
    Those most important things
Or was faith lost with the cynicism
    That unbridled knowledge brings?
I speak to you from a distant day
    And from dark, uncertain times;
Is there a message here for you
    In my silly little rhymes?
Love God and Jesus, your family,
    And love your country, too;
America needed us in our time long ago
    And today she depends on you!

God bless you and God bless America!

September 17, 2002

---

## Inscription on a Plaque

The names placed upon this wall
    And raised up from this plaque
Are people who got something good
    And gave a whole lot back.
And if you spoke to each of them
    Their answers would be the same,
"The camp is for the boys,
    Don't worry about my name!"
What brought these folks together
    So they could do this deed?
It was a common way of thinking,
    The Scout Oath helped them succeed.
Duty to God and Country
    And to their fellow man,

To help a person grow up right
    Was a big part of their plan.

The years have passed and so have some
    With names upon this wall;
So who will help this camp to grow?
    For they can no longer do it all.
The destiny of our nation,
    Indeed the fate of our whole earth,
Depends on people just like you
    Knowing what it's worth.
There are generations yet to come
    Who you will never know
But I did not see you standing there
    When I wrote these words so long ago.
Yet the words serve to remind you
    That we were here indeed
And ask you please to carry on
    For it's now your turn to lead.

In honor of Jorge Verduzco, Ian Imrie, Joe Galbraith and John Thurston
in establishing Camp Huisache in Laredo, Texas

## Chapter Three

# Our Llamas
# Are Not Camels

## *Our Llamas Are Not Camels*

"What can these llamas do," I asked,
  "I'm taking an exotic trip.
I need one to carry burdens
  And one whose feet don't slip."
The salesman rubbed his chin and said,
  "Sir, all our llamas have special gifts,
This one's climbed the highest peaks
  And three times his weight he lifts!"
"Yes, that's all so well and good," I said,
  But for this trip I need something more.
Can these llamas go without water
  For a week on the desert floor?"
The salesman scratched his head a bit
  Then looked deep into my eyes;
"Sir," he said, "I won't say they can
  For I do not trade in lies.
Our llamas are not camels, sir,
  Though for llamas they're built well
But if you need a camel,
  I don't have a one to sell.
Our llamas are made for mountain trails,
  Not deserts don't you see?

Would you take God's special gift for you
    And then find something else to be?
You're like a llama in the desert
    When you misuse that gift of yours,
For a llama's only like a camel
    In that it spits a lot and snores!"

## These Geese Don't Fly on Tuesdays

The sun was setting that Tuesday eve
    As I neared the mountain top
But even with my lack of time
    The scene before me made me stop.
A giant waterfall
    Was dammed completely dry;
Geese that should be flying south
    Wouldn't flap their wings to fly.
The trail that led to the highest peak
    Was blocked by a giant gate;
A sign on the nearby cabin said,
    "He who knocks, must wait."
"Hello," I called, "What's happened here?"
    "Is everything okay?"
I never saw the man inside
    But here's what I heard him say:
"These geese don't fly on Tuesdays,
    The fish don't swim after eight;
We never take a chance here,
    If we do, we're always late.
The waterfall doesn't run in summer,
    We don't harvest grain in fall;

We find that if we don't water them,
    These trees don't grow at all.
We don't have leaves to rake,
    We never have grass to mow;
There's nothing that we want to learn,
    We know all there is to know.
I won't climb that mountain
    And I won't take that trail;
I won't try a thing that's new,
    That way I'll never fail."
The woods were strangely silent
    And the air was dead to sound;
The flowers that once had bloomed here
    Returned to barren ground.
The best thing I could do
    Was to leave that man in peace,
But I threw a rock as I climbed the trail
    And off flew all the geese.

## March of the Sea Turtles

You'd think they'd learn after all these years
    But there they go again,
Sea turtles digging holes in sand
    To lay their eggs all in.
Soon the time will come to hatch
    And for the young to seek the sea,
Yet birds will eat most all of them
    For they have but fins to flee.
The turtles that survive that march
    Should think of something better;

Instead of laying eggs in sand
    They should find a place much wetter.
But they'll never change the things they do
    No matter how many young are lost,
Yet unlike people who act the same
    The turtles can't count the cost.

---

## Invasion of the Woodpeckers

I listened to the woodpecker
    As it knocked upon the tree;
Knowing that it ate parasites
    Was comforting to me.
I was delighted when two of them
    Flew over from next door
But did not know what to do
    When I saw a hundred more.
The sky was dark with woodpeckers,
    The trees were shaking with their blows;
By spring these ravaged trees would die
    For with such damage nothing grows.
The woodpeckers kept on pecking
    After all the bugs and bark were gone;
They kept on sinking holes all night
    And there were more of them by dawn.
The invasion of the woodpeckers
    Is an awesome, dreadful sight
And the next time you stop to criticize,
    Remember it you might.

---

## It's Not Just Ivy

I met a boy the other day,
    A brave and daring soul;
He snuck into the watermelon patch,
    To steal the biggest was his goal.
"I know all about watermelons," he said
    As his chest swelled up with pride,
"I'll thump each one in that patch
    To tell which is the best inside."
"I'm so smart," that's what he said,
    A boy proud of what he knows,
But there was poison ivy in the patch
    And now his knowledge shows.
He did just as he said he would
    And he never did get caught
But God and nature had conspired
    And this lad a lesson taught.

---

## The Smallest Malamute

I don't think he understood
    That he was not sized like all the others
But this little malamute
    Could walk under his sisters and brothers.
His view of life never got
    More than six inches off the floor
And though in play he was often tossed
    He always came back for more.
Yes, inside that tiny body
    Was a heart big as could be
And though outnumbered and outsized
    He often made his opponents flee.

His short and stubby legs
    And his body stretched so long
Would remind you of a dachshund
    But his bark would say, "You're wrong!"
For courage can't be measured
    By ones's build or lack of size;
That's what the smallest malamute
    Helped me realize.

---

## Sinbad and the Shining Pyramid

He cupped it in his hands
    And its light filled the giant room;
Sinbad had found the treasure
    That brought so many to their doom.
Years he searched the ruins
    Of crypts and temples great;
Elated now that it was his
    And he'd escaped their awful fate.
He left behind his family
    And sold his goods and lands
But now all that seemed little
    Because he held it in his hands.
The pyramid gave a burst of light
    So he quickly hid his eyes
But in his sudden fear and haste
    Sinbad dropped his costly prize.
Smashed in a thousand pieces,
    Broken on the floor,
Sinbad's prize was worthless
    And didn't shine anymore.
What will you give for riches?
    What makes you think you're wise?

And will you trade your life away
    For what disappears before your eyes?
The road is wide that leads that way
    But it is not too late
For you can follow Jesus now
    And go in by the narrow gate.

## Chapter Four

# Grandma's
# Christmas China

### *Grandma's Christmas China*

She bought it for their first Christmas,
    They were so young back then,
And when she looks into the china
    I think she sees his face again.
She trembles and lifts her hand
    To cover a sudden gasp;
This year he won't be with her
    And the china escapes her grasp.
It's only a single plate
    That's fallen to the floor
But the tears fall down like rain
    For she's lost a whole lot more.
They spent a lifetime lost in love,
    These two had become one pair;
And her life's in shattered pieces
    Just like the dinnerware.
Then somewhere from deep inside her
    She hears a familiar voice
And she starts to pick up the pieces
    For Grandma has made her choice.
The grandkids are coming over,
    She knows that dinner just won't wait,
So she sets out the food and china
    Missing only one broken plate.

For Marjorie

━━━⟨∞⟩━━━

## The Mouse and the Plate of Cookies

It was on that cold and quiet night
  In that house you've read about before
But the mouse that wasn't stirring
  Wasn't sleeping anymore.
A tiny angel woke him
  To give an important task,
"Guard the cookie plate for Santa,"
  Was all she had to ask.
Now that may not seem important
  To creatures big and tall
But a promise is a promise
  Even for a mouse so small.
The mouse sat by the cookie plate
  And gave his hunger no heed
But he did toss down a cookie
  When he saw the cat in need.
Another cookie was given
  To a child up for a drink;
He saw the parakeet had no food
  And he didn't stop to think.
Before the night was over
  All the cookies disappeared
And the mouse was very frightened
  As the sound of sleigh bells neared.
Down the chimney came Santa
  Into that quiet house;
He saw the empty plate
  And the tiny little mouse.
"Santa, I'm sorry," said the mouse,
  His tiny voice was filled with shame,

"I gave all your cookies away
  And I'm the only one to blame.
I was put in charge of them
  And the night did seem so long;
I gave them all to those in need,
  I wish I had been strong."
Santa nodded gently
  And whispered a soft "Ho, ho!"
"What you say reminds me
  Of a story long ago.
A man who saved His people
  Went to heaven to prepare a place;
He left with them His Spirit
  To fill them all with grace.
He wanted them to share their things
  As He had done and said,
Just as you, my little one,
  Have all these others fed.
You have fulfilled your promise;
  You have kept your word!
I hope that others act like you
  When this story they have heard."
Then Santa left the gifts he brought
  For all the people of the house,
Each of whom would do quite well
  To follow the example of the mouse.

---

## Christmas Collection

Grandpa's fingers weren't nimble
  Even as a younger man
But he wrapped the presents he gave with love
  As only grandpas can.

So when he sent me to the attic
  To bring down some boxes stored up there,
I was surprised to see such gentle hands
  Open each one with deliberate care.
"Grandma had this collection
  Since she was twenty-two;
She added one more house each year
  And she wants it to go to you."
Grandpa told me a Christmas story
  About each house that Grandma treasured
And Grandpa's hands showed his love
  For in such ways these things are measured.
Grandpa spent so much time
  To put them back just as they were
So the houses like their love
  Would live on and endure.
"Remember this is how Grandma said
  They must be put away."
"Yes Grandpa, I'll remember that"
  And all the things you didn't have to say.

---

## *The Secrets of the - Shhhh!*

I'm hoping I can get this down
  Disguised in rhyme and verse
Or else they could kick the cat,
  Pull her tail or something worse!
You see, I saw them yesterday
  As they hid to spy
And to keep their secret
  There's not a thing they wouldn't try.
They are Santa's helpers,
  Oh, they started long ago,

But they've been silent all these years
    So only old folks know.
Yes, you've heard of the bearded ones,
    Those who stock the shelves,
But who does Santa use to spy,
    A bunch of big fat elves?
No, he uses smaller sneaky ones,
    Deception is their game,
They make the list of naughtiness,
    The brownies, that's their name.
I tried to tell their secret
    And the truth about them air;
But they can be real naughty too,
    It's not just the cat they scare!
That's why I'm in the library,
    I could not write this in the house;
The brownies are all watching there,
    Quieter even than a mouse.
They are thin and crafty
    And stand less than one foot two;
My father said when he was small
    He once felt one in his shoe!
His brother saw one at the glass,
    Brownies trimmed their Christmas tree,
But now I've told their secret.
    Oh what will become of me?
I can't type this on computer,
    The brownies know a virus;
I'll have to write it out in blood
    On a sheet of old papyrus!
Shhhh! Look, over there!
    I can't see it but I heard!
So if this story gets to you,
    Hush! Don't say a word!

## Our Llamas Can Be Reindeer

"Our llamas are not camels, sir,
　　But they can pull a sleigh.
Perhaps you need a llama
　　To serve as a reindeer today?"
Now Santa had tried everything,
　　Even a reindeer with a glowing nose,
And somehow no matter what
　　That old red sleigh still goes.
But Cupid had a wounded heart
　　And Comet had to be scrubbed;
Dancer had to sit this one out
　　Because his hoof was stubbed.
Even with Rudolf in the lead
　　Santa was still two deer short,
So when he got two llamas
　　The reindeer didn't snort.
"Put some antlers on them," said Santa,
　　Talking to his elves,
"If we sprinkle them with pixie dust
　　They can learn to fly themselves!"
Instead of Comet and Cupid
　　Santa called, "Juanita! Jose!"
And that night was the first
　　That two llamas pulled his sleigh.
Yes, it's hard to imagine
　　Llamas floating in the sky
But until you heard of Santa
　　Did you really think reindeer could fly?
For llamas can be as reindeer
　　And give Santa's sleigh a lift
Since Christmas is for everyone
　　Who receives God's special gift.

———— ⊶⊷ ————

## Christmas Cash

It came in the mail from Grandma
    With a note from her that read:

"You're old enough to choose,
    That's what your parents said;
I would have liked to choose for you
    But I'm sending this instead.
How you use it is up to you,
    You can save or you can spend,
But what you do is important
    For it WILL matter in the end.
You can spend it on yourself,
    For this gift is meant for you,
On the things that make you happy
    And for what you like to do.
You can give it to a worthy cause,
    And make your heart feel warm inside;
Choose wisely who you give it to,
    Let Jesus be your guide.
You can save it for a rainy day
    Or begin to build a nest,
For as much as I would like to help
    You alone must take life's test.
So make your choices wisely
    And your gifts will take you far;
Now, with the love I send with this,
    Reach up and touch a star!"

———— ⊶⊷ ————

## My Doll

Here's a picture when she was five
    Next to the Christmas tree,
Holding a doll as big as her
    As tight as tight could be.
In photographs this family
    Looks the same as any other
But life was not a picture book
    For her, her sister, or brother.
Holding that big doll she has
    The most determined pair of eyes
As though she's found a treasure
    And she's fixed on that one prize.
Now here's a later photograph,
    On the back I see her name,
Of a mother and her baby
    And the look is just the same.
She loved that doll as a little girl,
    She washed it with her tears,
But the dream that started with the doll
    Came true after all these years.
Yes, she suffered more than you and I
    Would ever care to know
But she hung on to her dream
    And never let it go.

---

## No Rocking Horse

On her Christmas list when she was five
    She put a rocking horse
But it wasn't there that morning,
    And she was so sad, of course.

She wouldn't even open
    The one small present she received;
She dreamed about that rocking horse
    And for its loss she grieved.
"I've been good all year long," she said,
    "I did really, really try."
She needed to know the answer
    So she asked her parents why.
"Open the gift you got from us,
    The reason's there," they said,
Inside the box she found a bridle
    And a note to her that read:
"No rocking horse for Christmas,
    So sad, not fair it seems,
But this bridle's for a real horse to ride
    On a trip beyond your dreams!
Child, don't be afraid to open
    All God's gifts to you.
When you look in every box,
    Far more than dreams come true!"

                For Erin

## Chapter Five

# No Shelter
# in Bethlehem

### No Shelter in Bethlehem

The air so cold, the wind so brisk,
    No shelter in Bethlehem tonight;
A mother's tears, His only warmth
    Until the morning light.
I would have been in Bethlehem
    To greet and welcome You
But I missed the signs the angels gave
    And only shepherds knew.
I would have given a place to sleep
    And songs before a fire;
Instead You faced the cold alone
    With only donkeys as a choir.
I would have given blankets
    To protect You from the wind
But I didn't see You coming
    And on me You could not depend.
Lord, how can You still love me?
    I've failed time and time again;
I missed the chance to celebrate
    Because of where my hands and heart have been.

The lightning strikes, the thunder rolls,
    It storms in Jerusalem tonight;
There's warmth in the blood of Jesus,
    As His followers take flight.

I would have spoken up for You
    But I was afraid to die;
I said I'd protect You, Lord,
    But I didn't even try.
I would have said I know You
    But my fears got the best of me;
I said I'd stay with You till the end
    But I took the chance to flee.
I would have believed You'd rise again
    But they put You in the grave;
What made You want to die for me
    For who was I to save?
Lord, I do not understand
    But I know Your love's so great.
Can you take me with You now?
    Please say it's not too late.

The air so fresh, the sea so blue,
    There's life in Galilee tonight;
There's warmth in my heart to welcome Him
    And finally set things right.
I have come to Galilee
    To listen to my Saviour speak;
I heard it from the shepherds
    And now I salvation seek.
I have bread to offer Him
    And with you I'll gladly share,
For I have seen the miracles
    And felt His loving care.
I have words to speak for Him
    And hands to do good deeds;
I have feet to follow Him
    Any place He leads.
Lord, I feel Your love for me,
    And return that love I do;
I will live so that those who watch
    In seeing me, see only You.

## Tale of the Cross

Another day, another body
    To stretch across and nail to me,
Just one more person to hold up high,
    His suffering for all to see.
This one needed help, he did,
    To even get me to the hill;
I wonder what things he did
    To make them want to kill.
He flinches like the others
    When they drive the nail into his hand
And I hear his muffled cries
    As they make his feet unfit to stand.
Why then does this one seem so strange
    As his blood pours over me?
For if I could, I'd stop them,
    And I would set him free.

We are joined, this man and I
    And soon we'll both be dead;
"My God why have you forsaken me,"
    Were the final words he said.
I've heard others' dying words
    And they were much like this,
But now I'm feeling different;
    What in him did I miss?
He's taken down and buried now
    But this feeling's very queer;
It's like he lives inside of me,
    How can he still be here?
I was dead until he touched me,
    I felt his final breath;

Was this man the Son of God,
  The One who would beat death?

My roots are firmly planted
  And they'll never chop me down;
I have seedlings planted everywhere
  And I'm the tallest tree in town.
Children climb my branches
  And old folks sleep in my shade;
Jesus shed His blood on me
  And from a cross, a tree was made.
They did not believe it
  And they said it wasn't true
But if Jesus did all this for me,
  What will He do for you?
Yes, I was the cross that held Him
  And you're the one who drove the nails;
Thank Jesus He's forgiven us
  With a love that never fails.

---

## Blind

Panic!
Terror!
Flight!
  The sudden blow takes me into endless night,
Into a realm where darkness reigns,
  Body and soul now bound in chains,
Praying, "Lord, please not too late
  Jesus save me from my awful fate!
A punishment I well deserve,
  Oh, that I may on this earth it serve.
Blinded, now only do I see
  The beauty of Your gift to me:

Freedom from the pains of sin,
   No price to pay, just ask You in."
Years of stumbling through clouded eyes,
   Fixed now on one holy prize:
Follow Jesus on the only way,
   Never more again to stray.

Clouds and fog give way to light
   For Jesus has restored my sight!
On this earth's beauty I still gaze;
   I give Him thanks and sing His praise.
I've seen now where I'd have been
   Had Jesus not rescued me from sin.
With sight He's also given voice
   To call to you to make a choice:
Life in darkness, suffering, pain,
   A soul in torment's constant strain;
Freedom for that soul to soar
   For all that's broken He will restore.
You stand alone now at that door,
   Knock and hear the heavens roar!

---

## Spirit Cloud

The fog bank filled the valley
   And its shape mirrored that of the hill,
But with the rising of the sun,
   Disappear it will.
At first I thought it spirit-like,
   Mysterious and gray,
But of body and of spirit,
   Which will most likely stay?

For at death the body's taken,
  Buried and is gone,
But with Jesus' love to carry it
  The spirit lives on and on.
Is your spirit like a cloud,
  To disappear with the blowing wind?
Or is it like a mountain,
  Built strong that knows no end?

———— ∞ ————

## Fill My Cup

Open my eyes, Lord, that I might see
  Injustice, hatred and poverty.
Do not let me hide my frightened eyes
  And miss the hungry child that cries;
Neither let me blink and miss
  The laughter, joy and the bliss
Poured out from those who live and love,
  Who share their gift from God above.

Open my ears, Lord, that I might hear
  The cries of anguish, fright and fear
Of the small, the weak, the poor;
  God help me now, I must do more.
Let me hear the angels sing
  And Your Word to all men bring;
Let me hear You clear and strong,
  I want to listen all day long.

Open my mouth, Lord, that I may speak
  And somehow turn the other cheek
When my words are wrongly turned around
  Yet find the strength to stand my ground

So those who laugh and those who doubt
    Will marvel as I rise and shout.
Lord, give me Your voice to use today
    So they'll cast their doubt and sins away.

Open my heart, Lord, that I may love
    And be filled with Spirit from above.
Fill me with all that's wholesome and good
    And help me desire the things that I should.
Fill me so full that I may dare
    In every deed show Your loving care
And on my final earthly day
    Give me strength to kneel and pray.

Open my hands, Lord, so that I might do
    Everything like You want me to.
Open them wide so Your love may pour,
    All You have given me and then give me more
So Your love from me like a river will flow
    In all of my deeds and wherever I go.
I'll give love to others as You've given to me
    And lose my life for You as You've set me free.

---

## Are You Next?

Are you next in the manger,
    Who will follow the king?
After the shepherds and wise men
    What is left to bring?
The angels have returned to heaven
    And the star has disappeared;
All the traces of that time are gone
    And the manger cleaned and cleared.

So why is it that you tarry here,
  Is it His presence you still feel?
For I, like they, would worship Him
  And I too would gladly kneel.
So I will listen for the angels
  Though they sing from far above
And my gifts I'll give to those in need
  Along with Jesus' love.

Are you next inside the temple?
  Do they let you in the gate?
If you want to hear the young man speak
  I'm afraid you are too late.
The words he spoke astounded them,
  The boy can fashion more than wood,
And I might make a difference here
  If talk like Him I could.
How can the son of a carpenter
  Speak with so much truth?
And how is it such learned men
  Know less than this simple youth?
The path to God is through righteousness
  And in following His ways
So I'll listen when this young man speaks
  And watch Him when He prays.

Are you next to take the basket?
  It grows heavy with each turn
For there are strange things happening
  So listen, watch and learn.
Do you have the faith
  Of a tiny mustard seed?
Then take an empty basket
  For there are hungry folks to feed.
Do you believe your eyes
  Like the blind man who now can see?

Then do like this man Jesus
  Who sets captive spirits free.
Can you walk on water?
  I think the grass will do,
To help others find the path
  For they depend on you.

Are you next upon the cross
  To suffer and to die,
To see your family torn apart
  And watch your mother cry?
With each fleeting breath
  You have one less to swallow
And it is not an easy life
  This dying man to follow.
But follow Him I will
  And I will lift my cross
For in dying I will live again
  And achieve gain in place of loss.
The cross of death I carry
  No longer troubles me
For in His resurrection
  Christ Jesus set me free.

Are you next in heaven?
  Yes, I'm very close somehow
For I can feel His Spirit;
  He lives inside me now.
Oh, I still walk the paths of earth
  And its dangers I still face
But I have naught to fear
  For He's given me His grace.
Yes the day is coming
  When these eyes shall see no more
For I'll need perfect eyes to see the light
  When they open heaven's door.

And with perfect eyes of your own
    You'll see me coming through
For a perfect sight of heaven
    Needs both me and you.

---

## No Relief in Sight

The battle's raging and we fall from the fight
    As hope is dying with no relief in sight
Yet I look above to that distant hill
    For I know there is Your great power still.
And though I don't hear Your trumpets yet call
    I'll fight on in faith and give it my all.
I'll never give up and I'll never give in
    Whatever I face, with You I will win.
I'll hold out against them with all of my might,
    I'll live and I'll die by doing what's right.
Evil surrounds me; I'd be filled with fear
    But my heart is a fortress for somehow You're here.
For try as they might they can't take me yet
    I'm on solid ground with my feet firmly set.
Let them come for me now, I'll die if I must
    I am ready my Lord, for in You is my trust.

---

## The Toy Bugle

A thousand trumpets lifted
    To call upon the king,
A thousand angels ready
    To fly on feathered wing,

Every angel blew a horn
But not a sound was made
And for people waiting on the earth
All hope began to fade.
Gabriel called to all his captains
And they quickly gathered round.
"What do we have to do," he asked,
"To make these trumpets sound?"
Only one could answer,
"Sir, I've found a way.
Before these trumpets make a noise
A human must first play."
So the angels went to orchestras
And every jazz and concert hall
But musicians couldn't play a note
Though they tried to, one and all.
In final desperation
The angels gathered once again.
"Who can play these trumpets," asked they,
"If not these strongest men?"
"Who shall inherit earth?" asked Gabriel,
"The meek ones and the mild.
Go forth and listen on the earth
For music from a child."
And though the angels listened
Not a note was heard
And only one angel was still gone
When they again conferred.
"There is no hope and all is lost!"
Their meeting was adjourned,
But then the one last angel came
To tell them what he'd learned.
"I traveled far and wide," he said,
To every lake and hill,
On one I thought I heard a note
So I listened, very still."

The angels were all hopeful
When he brought forth a little boy
Until they looked and saw
That his bugle was a toy.
They held him to a mouthpiece
But it was bigger than his head;
The little boy just laughed out loud,
"I'll play mine instead!"
He stood up straight and tall
And held his bugle high
And from that tiny bugle
Came a noise that split the sky!
A thousand trumpets sounded
And sparkled in the sun
But the tiny little bugle
Was still the loudest one.
It doesn't take a giant
To be herald to the king
But it sometimes takes a person
To help the angels sing.
For angels only finish
What human hands must start
And nothing is impossible
With Jesus in your heart.

For Gene, the bugler.

—⊶⊷—

## Chapter Six

# Blackberry Jam

### Blackberry Jam

I still taste it after all these years
 Though Mom's grandma's long since gone;
She made the best blackberry jam
 No matter what I put it on.
I covered every piece of bread
 Until the cupboard was almost bare;
My little sister once made a mess
 And I licked it from her hair.
My mom still has the recipe,
 She's the only one who knows it;
She learned to cook from her grandma
 And I'm afraid my waistline shows it.
Still there was something in the jam back then
 That recipes can't measure;
The simpler love of a simpler time
 Is a thing I'll always treasure.
And when my children taste their grandma's jam
 Their eyes are shining bright;
For them like me so long ago
 She makes that jam just right!

## Saturday Rules

"Stop!" exclaimed my five-year-old,
  "You cannot go out this door!
I just passed a law for daddies:
  No working Saturdays anymore."
I had some extra time
  To research this new found law
And to look at the world a different way,
  To see as my five-year-old saw.
"You get up early every day,
  You leave before I wake;
You don't have time to read to me
  Or see the pictures that I make.
Santa will be coming soon,
  If you break this law then you'll be bad,
And if I ever break a rule like that
  It makes Mommy really mad."
He stood there firmly by the door
  With his hands upon his hips
And I could see that he was serious
  By the tightness in his lips.
I laughed and hugged him snugly,
  Glad to let him win,
And called and told the office,
  "I won't be coming in."

For Ryan

---

## Chess with Grandpa

My grandpa taught me to play chess
  When I was nine or ten;

Grandpa would show me my mistakes
    And sometimes let me win.
Grandpa always played with black
    So I started out with white;
I liked to use my bishops
    But Grandpa preferred the knight.
Grandpa would often lay a trap;
    I attacked with moves quite bold,
Two ways to try to win at chess,
    Two players, one young, one old.
Yet there was always so much more to it
    Than who could win a game
For though we played opposing sides
    Our love was still the same.
And in a future years from now
    I'll play a match with my grandson
And even if I lose that game
    Grandpa and I will both have won.

---

## Forgive Me

Forgive me, my old friend,
    I know I've done you wrong;
I should have asked you way back then
    And now it's been so long.
We haven't spoken since then,
    It's been so many years,
And yes I am full of doubt
    And those unspoken fears.
Will you yet remember
    The wrong I did to you?

And though it happened long ago
    Does the pain still burn like new?
Did you carry the burden far?
    Can you now finally let it rest?
For though I let you down
    I see you passed the test.
I pray that God has held you up
    And that to you He will be true,
That now at last after all these years
    I can make it up to you.

## Safe at Home

He grew up hearing baseball
    With the stadium just blocks away;
His father took all his boys
    To watch the home team play.
He wore a Cardinals uniform,
    They were his favorite of all the teams;
My father just loved baseball
    And it loved him too, it seems.
He bought us each a radio
    The nightly game to hear;
Baseball and his love for us,
    That message, loud and clear.
Lou Gehrig's took him from us
    And made his life too short a run
But not before his team came back
    And another championship won.
The home that he grew up in
    And that old ball field both are gone
But Dad now lies forever
    Next to a newer diamond lawn.

Baseball, a game for little boys to play
    That reminds them when they're men,
Life may take you far away
    But it'll bring you home again.

        For Clyde, Hermann, Charles and baseball.

---

## The Big Blue Recliner

I remember it like it was yesterday,
    The children were one and three;
When we were tired and ready for bed
    They would sleep in the recliner with me.
I would rock us to sleep with a child in each arm,
    I remember the scent of their hair;
When Momma came back from her work at night
    She would find us sleeping there.
Carefully, gently, she would lift each child
    And quietly take them to bed
But I would awake for my children were gone
    And I was holding thin air instead.
I sang them to sleep, seems like just last night
    And I told them a story too;
It must have been long for they're both tall now
    And the story was only just through.
Time doesn't let us stay the same
    And the world allows no rest;.
Children grow up way too fast
    And hurry to give life a test.
But they will remember as will I
    The comfort we all felt there
And the peace that came over us
    As we slept in the reclining chair.

        For Carol

## The Watch

It was his grandfather's watch I'm told,
    On its cover is a name,
And though I do not know the first
    The last one is the same.
I turn the key that winds the watch,
    One full and again for two;
My father gave this watch to me
    And I will pass it on to you.
You have the name that's written there,
    You must see it every day;
Things go with the name that like the watch
    Should not be cast away:
Tell the truth despite the cost
    And always do what's right;
Know when it's best to compromise
    And when you have to fight.
Pray to God for guidance
    And in Jesus put your trust;
Love those in your family
    For sacrifice you must.
Enjoy all life has to give
    And be happy every day;
When those around are lost,
    Look and find the way.
The watch will run for three more months
    Now that I've wound it so;
These things take with you all your life
    Wherever you may go.

## *Grandpa*

He was the only boy of seven children
  And at ten his father died.
It was a cold winter's day in Maine
  And the tears froze as he cried.
He was born a hundred years ago
  In a world and time that's flown
Yet his independent spirit
  Gives me strength as yet unknown.
In winter when he went to sleep
  A hot brick warmed his feet
And he had to walk to school
  In rain and snow and sleet.
In summertime he slept alone
  In a shed just down the trail
And sometimes with his friends
  He took a free ride on the rail.
I see this picture of him
  With his cousin riding bikes
And here's one on Katahdin
  With that special girl he likes.

A different time, a different place
  But the challenge still the same
For a young man heading out
  Into the world to make a name.
Not knowing what lay ahead of him
  Yet sure of self inside,
A growing faith to carry him
  And a little bit of pride.
He needed every bit of it
  For tragedy befell:
Both his sons he lost in youth
  And of his pain I cannot tell.
But I do know that his family held
  In times of awful stress

And when I face tough times
   I will do nothing less.
And though you did now know him
   And the world knows not his name,
Grandpa's living large
   In our family's Hall of Fame.

For my grandfather, Alonzo Taylor, and for yours.

---

## *Dear Mr. Jesus*

Grant me a daddy, Mr. Jesus please,
   Who will get on the floor and play on his knees;
I want his face close but I'm not tall yet
   And when I'm older I'm afraid I'll forget.
I might not remember how I felt today
   When Daddy laughed and said he could stay;
We played with my animals and we all had tea
   But the only ones who could drink it were Daddy and me.
I helped him outside when he worked in the yard
   I watered the grass—and Daddy—that wasn't too hard.
We went out to eat, there's a playground there;
   Daddy got stuck but he didn't care.
We went back home and I sat on his lap
   We were sleepy so we both took a nap;
When I woke up I was back in bed
   And Daddy was sitting there patting my head.
I held out my arms and he hugged me tight;
   He told me my friend could come over tonight.
We went outside then and rode our new bikes;
   We played baseball, and Daddy, he gave me four strikes!
Daddy cooked hamburgers out on the grill;
   I want to remember, I promise I will!

Help Daddy remember please too,
  He sometimes forgets things, between me and you!
Thank you, Mr. Jesus, for my wish today
  And for such a good daddy, let me keep him, I pray.

---

## A Moment in Time

Grant me dear Lord, a moment in time,
  A day to ignore the alarm clock chime,
A morning that though I can lie in bed
  I wake to watch what's happening instead,
Some coffee to sip as I see the sunrise,
  The love of my wife as I kiss sleepy eyes.
Grant me a day, Lord, when I say all things right
  And lullabies to sing to my children tonight.
Help me live life like the blue sky today
  And grant any dark clouds be swept away.
Grant just one day, Lord, of joyful bliss
  And I will try to make all my days like this:
A day that I listen, a time to be heard,
  Quiet moments to spend reading Your Word.
Grant me the power to kiss away tears
  And when they are frightened, to calm children's fears.
Some time today let us play in the sun
  And just for once not put a clock on our fun.
Bring a bit of heaven down to the earth
  And join with us, Lord, in unbridled mirth.
Grant us this day, Lord, with no earthly care
  And that wherever we go, Lord, You'll always be there.

---

## The Parakeet

They bought it at the pet shop,
    This little parakeet;
Like their love it was young
    And its melody so sweet.
But the years had worn that love
    So it wasn't like before
And she told him that she had to leave;
    She didn't love him anymore.
They divided all the things
    They'd won and bought together;
When it came down to the parakeet
    She wouldn't touch a feather.
"You can have it, I don't care,
    But I think you should let it go;
Trapped inside that cage of yours
    It never had a chance to grow."
"What you call a cage," he said,
    "We once both called a nest
And we could both be free in love
    If we would each just give our best."
He had done all he could
    But he knew he couldn't make her stay
And though he kept the parakeet,
    She took his heart and flew away.

---

## The Long Good-bye

We live in the same house under the same roof;
    We're often close yet sometimes aloof.
I remember playing on the floor
    And how they'd meet me at the door

When I came home from work to play
    But no one greets me here today.
He's got his own things he likes to do
    And she has interests she'd like to pursue.
So where does daddy fit anymore?
    Its not the same, not like before.
A minute here, an answer there,
    Say the wrong thing and face that angry stare.
But wait, now he's hugging me,
    The love's still there but I didn't see.
They're doing what we coached and taught,
    They're choosing the paths they so long have sought.
No, he's no longer a little boy
    And she's grown up from that bundle of joy.
One day too soon they'll be out my door
    And they won't live here anymore.
It's a long good-bye we're embarking on
    And on that first day when they're both gone
I'll shed some tears for my wife and me
    But I'll thank God they grew up free.
I'll remember well the little boy and girl
    I lifted together to spin and whirl.
But I'll remember these teen years too,
    When those little ones changed and grew
Becoming the adults that you will know;
    Oh, God I'll be sorry to see them go.
The day is coming, it's drawing nigh,
    For these teenage years are the long good-bye.

---

## Chapter Seven

# Ours for Keeps

## Ours for Keeps

I stood in the yard looking up at my dad
    For I had to give an important speech;
I spoke with all the courage a three-year-old could,
    "Daddy, we need a puppy to love and to teach."
My dad looked down with a smile in his eyes,
    He said, "Okay son, we'll see.
I'm sure there's a puppy that needs a home
    And we'll pick one out, you and me."
"Ours for Keeps" was our puppy dog's name,
    Not Snoopy or Fido or Spot,
And the love my daddy showed me that day
    Is something I never forgot.

Ours for Keeps would pull on a rope
    And bark if you held it up high.
Mom would call, "Give that dog his rope!"
    "But it's Ours for Keeps'!" we would cry.
Old folks would smile when they asked his name;
    "It's Ours for Keeps," we would say.
"I just want to know his name," they'd reply,
    "I don't want to take him away!"
My daddy would tell the dog at night,
    "Protect that boy as he sleeps,
For just like you, my canine friend,
    He too is 'ours for keeps.'"

I grew up with Ours for Keeps
  And he grew old as I did;
He heard me argue with Dad sometimes
  For I was no longer a kid.
I had my own ideas to try
  And we didn't see things the same,
But there was one thing that kept us close
  And Ours for Keeps was his name.
We hugged and cried on his final day,
  When losing such friends one weeps,
But the love that dog gave the two of us
  Will always be "Ours for Keeps."

---

## *Grant*

Grant me, dear Lord, a little child,
  A beautiful baby to hold for a while.
Lord help me remember—everything—
  Each step, each word, the first ride on the swing.
Grant that my child gladly greets each day,
  Come be with our family and with all of us stay.
Grant that a good parent I will be
  And my child's every need, Lord, please let me see.
Let me see times when I should stay near
  And teach me, Lord, how to listen and hear.
Grant me a day when I'll watch my child run
  And see my child laugh as the merry-go-round's spun.
Keep my child happy, healthy and safe above all
  And grant my child courage to heed when You call.
My baby will grow quickly, the time goes so fast,
  Help me grow too, Lord, yet remember the past
So I may know always the joy little ones bring
  From this moment on 'til the final bells ring.

Grant us this moment, Lord, grant us this gift,
  Grant us the wisdom prayerful hands to lift.
"Remember this little child and our happy days,
  Grant a life full of love and a heart filled with praise."

---

## True Friends

True friends never part
  And so we never will;
You'll be with me in heart and mind
  'Til all the clocks stand still.
And when great bards and poets
  Write of friendships grand
They'll surely tell of yours and mine,
  The deepest in all the land.

We've traveled far and wide
  For causes great and just;
God calls me on alone, my friend,
  My broken heart says go I must.
But though the miles divide us now
  Your smiling face still I see,
For distance cannot set apart
  Two friends like you and me.

You'll live in my heart forever
  And I in yours I know;
We will always be together
  No matter where we go.
And though the pain we're feeling
  Causes tears to fall,
The deeds we've done have made us strong,
  Together we've done it all.

God has plans for everyone,
    He caused our lives to touch
And the love we feel is His,
    It can never be too much.
And whene'er we meet on earth or heaven
    Our hearts will leap on high,
For true friends are forever
    Just like you and I.

    For my friend Joe Galbraith, Corpus Christi, Texas

———⌗———

## Children's Day

I knew we had a Mother's Day
    And all of us knew why
And of course there is a Father's Day
    Because of how hard they always try.
But we wanted a day just for us
    One we could call our own,
We decided to ask Daddy now
    And not wait 'til we were grown.
"Daddy, there's no Children's Day,
    Please won't you tell us why?"
"Every day is Children's Day!"
    Was my father's deep reply.
We didn't like the answer,
    No presents under a tree,
But my father lived out what he said
    In all he did for me.

It was Children's Day on holidays
    Spent together at the beach
And when we needed help at school
    Daddy always stopped to teach.

He held us on his shoulders,
    He lifted us one and all,
We could touch the sky from there,
    My God, he seemed so tall!
We hiked together on mountain trails,
    As we children changed and grew,
He led us to the path of life,
    Let us go and off we flew.
But to Dad it was still Children's Day
    And to that he held so true.
Can we make it Children's Day?
    It's up to me and you.

Is it Children's Day with wars and bombs
    That make children cry in pain,
Or when little ones are taken
    Leaving parents to call out in vain?
Look at me, I'm only one,
    What difference can I make?
I'll make it Children's Day today,
    There's just so much at stake.
I'll love my children with all my heart
    And give them time to spend
And when children anywhere need help
    My helping hand I'll lend.
"Every day is Children's Day,"
    My father said to me
And I will work to make it so,
    It's what was meant to be.

Can Children's Day survive
    Since my father's passed away?
The answer's in their laughter
    As the children run and play.
Their grandpa knew that play and fun
    Were cures for many ills

And that will help their parents too,
    So put down your work and bills.
Spend time now with your children
    To teach what's wrong and right
And tell them that you love them
    As you tuck them in tonight.
For our children are a treasure
    Who in our hearts will stay
When we cheer and celebrate
    Every day as Children's Day.

---

## Angel on a Pillow

I lift her head and lay it down
    On the pillow I put there
And I sit and watch her sleeping
    For I cannot help but stare.
Resting on a pillow
    So pure and white and soft,
She looks just like an angel
    Asleep in clouds aloft.
I run my fingers through her hair
    And her locks I gently comb,
Glad she rests her weary head
    In this place we both call home.
And now I lie beside her
    To hold her close and tight,
An angel on a pillow
    To love throughout the night.
And when I awake in morning
    Her face is what I see,
"My angel on a pillow,"
    She smiles and says to me.

For Sharon

## Hello Friend Across the Years

Hello Friend, I'd like to be
    But I just don't know what's become of me,
Have I passed away and gone to my rest?
    I hope you're not reading this for a test!
You probably have computers now
    That learn to write and rhyme somehow,
So how did you happen upon this book
    And what prompted you to take a look?
Are you using it now to hold the door
    Or does it rest upon the bathroom floor?
I'm glad it's found some use today
    Even if you don't read all that I say.
But here's an idea for you to try:
    Write a note in ink and let it dry.
Say something witty to future folks
    And hope they understand your ancient jokes.
Add your thoughts to the ones on this page
    And pass them on to another age.
Something simple and friendly will do
    To reach through time like I did for you.

Byron, October 25, 2002

## Chapter Eight

# Last Chance
# for the
# Big Purple Dog

### Last Chance for the Big Purple Dog

"Today's the day." "She needs a home."
　　The officers' tones were grim
For they'd come to love that purple dog
　　And she in turn loved them.
But who would take a purple dog,
　　With such color it can't be well.
And can purple dogs be vicious?
　　At that time no one could tell.
Time had all run out
　　And no one took her yet
And the officer hung his head
　　As he got the phone to call the vet.
"I have a purple dog," he said,
　　"I'll bring her over in the van."
"Oh good!" said the happy vet,
　　"For I know a purple man."
It isn't always obvious
　　Like one's furry-coated hue
But everyone needs a special friend
　　And God has one for you!

———∞———

## Jesus Does Dishes

The sink was full of dirty dishes
 Needing to be cleaned and put away.
"They'll be dirty again tomorrow," I thought,
 "No matter how clean they get today."
Indeed there were several bowls
 Taken from the washer just last night,
Dirtier now than ever before;
 Man, that's just not right!
I wonder what Jesus thinks
 When He has to clean us up again;
"When will these people ever learn
 The cost of all this sin?"
Does Jesus ever tire like I do
 When the dishes pile too high?
And when He looks at all that dirt
 Does He shake his head and sigh?
Thank God He doesn't take days off
 When our lives again we've messed;
Still shouldn't we just do what's right
 And give our Lord a rest?

---

## Knocked Off

Jesus knocked me off my rocking horse!
 God, please make Him go away!
I like it here inside my room
 But He won't let me stay.
"You must leave the house," He said,
 "There's a surprise that waits for you."
So this thoroughbred that I now ride
 Must mean His words were true.

I thought I went so very fast
    On that tiny horse there in my room
But now I'm really moving
    As down the track we zoom.
I'll trust in Jesus every time
    He says that I am ready
So when He puts me in a spaceship
    I'll hold that rocket steady.
From rocking horse to rocket ship
    We've seen our friendship bond,
Now Jesus calls us onward
    To even greater things beyond.

In honor of Ryan Sample

---

## Dreams Are Dreams

Did you ever dream that you could fly,
    Or that you found a pot of gold?
I once had a dream like that
    When I was eight years old.
I flew high like Superman
    And saw the little cars below;
I knew that treasure was really real,
    I close my eyes and still can see it glow.
But dreams are dreams and real is real
    When I awoke it disappeared;
The chance to make a difference in the world
    Now also gone I feared.
But out of death He's given life to me
    And I look forward to each hour
For God can make your dreams come true;
    Indeed, He has that power.

My treasure lives in heaven now
  And I'll fly there when I go;
My dreams came true with Jesus
  And yours will too, I know.

---

## The Barnacled Walrus

He was the biggest fattest walrus
  So he pushed all the others around;
Instead of doing any work
  He just sat there on the ground.
He didn't even fish for food,
  Work was a stranger to his name,
And when he started growing barnacles
  That just added to his fame.
He perched atop the biggest rock
  To get the grandest view
And he got quite attached up there
  As the barnacles grew and grew.
A storm was brewing in the sea,
  The waves came crashing high;
Fierce winds lashed the beach
  And lightning flashed from the sky.
All the other walruses
  Swam to get away
But the walrus with his barnacles
  Was stuck and had to stay.
Are we like that walrus stuck
  With riches like barnacles grown
And will we call to God for help
  Or face the storm alone?

---

## The Tardy Whooping Crane

The frost had gathered on the grain,
    Winter winds were coming fast;
The whooping crane had tarried
    And of its flock it was the last.
As it flew it could see
    The leaves all fallen to the ground;
With the snowfall close behind
    It was finally southward bound.
"What will become of me
    And why did I leave so late?
I do not know what's ahead
    And now my task is great.
Are there any fish left
    To catch with my sharp bill?
And if they are all gone
    How will I my stomach fill?"
Yet the marsh had fish aplenty
    When it reached the coastal plain
And it had as much to eat
    As the early whooping crane.
Almost too late in leaving,
    The tardy whooping crane came through,
And God has room in heaven
    For a latecomer like you!

---

## Whose Home?

They live in the finest houses
    And in the humblest homes;
They hide out in your patio
    Underneath the garden gnomes.

They're always seeking cover
    To hide out from the light
And should anyone expose them
    They'll hurriedly take flight.
Carriers of germs and sickness,
    They quickly grow and breed;
Where there's one there are hundreds more,
    So homeowners take heed.
Your heart is a home for Jesus,
    Let's clean that one place well,
For you're adding one more cockroach
    With every lie you tell.

# Chapter Nine

# Soggy Buns

### Soggy Buns

I went into a restaurant
    To have a simple meal
Surprised to find inside my box
    Something awful to reveal.
No, it wasn't something living
    Or thin catsup as it runs
But the worst of all encounters:
    Hamburgers with soggy buns!
I couldn't even pick it up
    Without my hand becoming wet
And when I told the manager
    He said something I'll ne'er forget.
"Sir, we carefully craft each meal,
    We're well aware of what's inside;
We've always had these soggy buns
    And we serve each one with pride!.
I have soggy buns
    Each and every place I go;
I like my soggy buns
    And so does everyone I know!"
I was completely speechless
    And did not know what to do,
For I like my buns firm and dry
    And I think my wife does too!

# The Earthworms

As I went jogging along the street
    I looked down from the sun to my feet;
I saw an earthworm writhing in the heat
    And all down the block the same scene repeat.
I stopped my hurried jogging pass,
    Started tossing earthworms on the grass.
I picked them up one by one,
    Saved them from the scorching sun.
My neighbor said from his lawn chair,
    "Friend, what are you doing there?"
"Saving earthworms," was my reply,
    "On the pavement they'll dry out and die."
My neighbor looked both left and right,
    Said, "Friend, try as you might,
You can't possibly save all these earthworms today
    And what difference would it make anyway?"
I paused and looked into my neighbor's eyes;
    I said, "Neighbor, here's what you need to realize,
It made a difference to that—"
    SPLAT!
    My neighbor squashed the earthworm flat!
He smashed another with his shoe;
    Said, "Friend, there's something wrong with you.
I think you'd better go inside,
    It's hot out here and your brain is fried!"

## Earthworms II

I ventured out another day
    When my neighbor was away.
I picked an earthworm off the street
    And tossed him on the grassy peat.
The earthworm wriggled and twirled around,
    Tried to dig into the ground.
My neighbor drove up in his truck;
    I thought that worm was outta luck.
But my neighbor went in when he saw me;
    That worm now seemed lucky as could be.
He escaped my neighbor's heavy feet,
    Not that sorry fate to meet.
Sliding under damp moist bark,
    That worm was hidden in the dark
But birds have eyesight that's quite good
    And a robin lit on that wet wood.
I tried to scare him, 'twas too late;
    An earthworm lunch the robin ate.
My neighbor saw me running there
    Trying to give that bird a scare.
"Saving earthworms again?" he cried;
    "Oh no, not me!" I denied.
"You tried to take one from that bird!"
    "You're mistaken, neighbor, that's absurd!"
My neighbor's wife heard our talk,
    Stepped outside on her front walk.
She knelt down in her garden to work,
    Started to dig, then turned with a jerk.
"Honey," she said, "Here's what I read:
    Earthworms are good for our flower bed.
Go to the street and pick up a few;
    You wouldn't mind...WOULD YOU?"
My neighbor mumbled so I could barely hear
    But he blushed bright red as he said, "Yes dear."

———⊗⊗⊗———

## *Earthworms III*

One morning I rose before the sun
    Ready to start my morning run.
I saw my neighbor by the curb,
    Him I cared not to disturb
But I turned my head to take a look
    At all the earthworms that he took.
Some he brought to the garden to drop
    And the rest in his lunch pail so I said, "STOP!"
"What are you doing, you can't go on
    And put all these earthworms in your lunch pail or lawn.
Before you know it they'll be all gone
    And they can't taste that good to munch on!"
My neighbor laughed and flashed a smile,
    "I don't eat earthworms, that's not my style.
I take them from the street, that's true
    But not to save them like you do.
Some go in the garden, that's my wife's wish
    But I take them to the lake—to FISH!"
It was still early and I hadn't run
    But fishing really seemed like fun.
I got into my neighbor's truck
    And a new friendship we soon struck.
We fished all through that sunny morn
    With those earthworms so forlorn.
We didn't fight, we fished instead
    And to the fish the earthworms fed.
We depleted all the fishing stocks
    With just one earthworm in the box.
We took the worm back home that noon,
    Had to hurry for it'd dry out soon.

Filled an aquarium with dirt and moss
    And there we did that earthworm toss.
We ate the fish at the noontime meal
    And I wondered, "How'd those earthworms feel?
Stuck on hooks to drown and die,
    That's life at the bottom of the food supply."
My neighbor snapped his fingers, gave me a dish,
    Said, "You think too much, here, eat more fish!"

I still think too much, that hasn't changed,
    There's that worm who our friendship arranged.
He still lives inside that house of glass,
    He's fat now, a nice meal for a bass.
But a fish's stomach he'll never fill,
    My neighbor and I both feed him still
For like our friendship he's really grown
    And a better home he's never known.
Safe from crush of boot or staff
    Our earthworm serves to make us laugh.

---

## The Piranha's Dentist

"Open wide please, Mr. P,
    Oh, your teeth look very bad;
What have you been eating?
    When was the last checkup that you had?
Do you ever brush, sir?
    Your breath is anything but fresh.
What's this caught between your teeth,
    A little piece of flesh?
My, your teeth are sharp, sir,
    My finger has been cut;

I'm dripping blood into your mouth,
    I'd wash it out but—
OWWCH! You bit my hand off, sir,
    So now you'll have to pay!
I'll pull your teeth out one by one,
    You don't need them anyway.
Hey! You ate my other hand;
    What is wrong with you?
If I didn't trust you, sir,
    Our business would be through!"

"I see your appointment's over
    Mr. P, did it go well?
It looks as though your gums are bleeding;
    Shall I call the dentist in to tell?"

"Sad am I to tell you,
    The dentist won't hear your shout
But if you wait a moment
    I'm sure he'll be right out!"

---

## Super-Frog

He could leap over the dog house,
    It took just a single bound;
He hopped faster than a rabbit
    And he sure could cover ground.
He could snap his tongue and catch a bug
    Twenty feet away
And any kid who picked him up
    Was repelled by his awesome spray.
He was the biggest strongest frog
    The planet's ever seen;

His amphibious friends all envied him,
    That's why they're all still green.
He didn't have a thing to prove,
    For his fame was widely known,
But he wanted to stop a train like Superman
    To show how strong he'd grown.
He hopped down to the station
    To catch the nine o'clock.
He waited across the street
    To show off for his webbed-foot flock.
When the nine o'clock came rolling in
    He jumped high across the road
But not high enough to miss my car
    And I squashed him like a toad.
Super-Frog, oh, Super-Frog
    Why did it have to end like that?
In his epic last performance
    Super-Frog seemed a little flat.

For Lenora and Fred Richter

---

## Llama-Man

He was born with the face of a llama,
    One only a mother could love,
And his skin grew so leathery
    It felt just like a glove.
He has all the powers of the llama,
    He is nimble on his feet,
And he never uses knives or forks,
    He just has grain to eat.
He can climb the tallest mountains
    And breathe the thinnest air;

He can carry several hundred pounds
    And never really care.
He is always kind and helpful
    Anywhere he goes
But there is always someone
    Who makes fun of his big nose.
Oh, it seems so funny
    To laugh at other's features
For people can be the kindest
    Or cruelest of all God's creatures.
So be careful who you ridicule
    Lest you should make a gaffe
And yes, you'll know you've stepped in it
    When you hear the llama's laugh.

---

## Noah Zark

I knew a man named Edwin Zark,
    Got married and had a son;
Named the poor kid Noah
    On a whim to have some fun.
They filled his room with animals,
    Two of every kind,
And the kids at school teased him once
    But Noah didn't mind.
"I don't have real animals," he said,
    "Like in a zoo or in a park
But I'd be glad to be your friend,
    My name is Noah Zark!"
His house was always full
    Of friends who came to play;
They filled it like that famous boat
    Saying, "Let's go to Noah Zark's today!"

As he grew he fell in love
 As young folks do and can
But it did confuse the preacher
 When she said, "Noah Zark's my man!"
They were married happily
 For their love was true
And when they had a baby boy
 They named him Noah II.
The house they bought they painted
 The colors of the rainbow
For God had blessed their family too
 And they wanted folks to know.
Noah says when introduced,
 "I'm not he of biblical fame,
But for all the good it's done me,
 I'm glad Noah Zark's my name!"

---

## Connections

A first attempt at haiku (And the next to last poem of the book)

A fish jumps and lands.
 A bird dives into the wave.
The fish flies away.

# Epilogue

Several people have asked me how it is that I began writing so suddenly. As has been my style of late, I answered with a poem. This one's called "The Writer" and it is in fact the last poem of the book.

## The Writer

When I write a story
    Or better yet, a poem,
The words and rhymes just come to me
    As though I already know 'em.
And I sometimes can recall
    The cover of a book,
One I can't find on this earth
    No matter where I look!
And I wonder if someone reads to me
    At night when I'm asleep
And the story gets into my mind
    Though locked up very deep.
Then sometime when I'm awake
    And properly inclined,
The story that I heard that night
    Will pop into my mind.
I really can't explain it,
    How through all these thoughts I sift;
I know it is not me
    So I count it as a gift.
And if I receive a present,
    God says pass it on to you,
And with His help today
    That's exactly what I'll do!

I have continued to receive inspiration from the Holy Spirit and from the people and things around me. I am compiling poems now for a new book, *Climb the Red Mountain*, which I hope to publish soon. Your comments and suggestions are appreciated. God bless you!

# *Don't Feed the Seagulls*
## Order Form

❑ YES, I want _____ copies of *Don't Feed the Seagulls* at $ 11.95 each.

❑ YES, I am interested in having Byron von Rosenberg speak to my company, association, school, or organization. Please send information.

❑ YES, please inform me when *Climb the Red Mountain* and subsequent books are published.

**Postal orders:**   Red Mountain Creations
P.O. Box 172
High Ridge, MO 63049

**Telephone orders:** 1-866-SEAGULS (1-866-732-4857)

**Website:** www.byronvonrosenberg.com

**Please send *Don't Feed the Seagulls* to:**

Name: _____

Organization: _____

Address: _____

City: _____ State: _____ Zip: _____

Telephone: (_____) _____

E-mail: _____

My check or money order for $_____ is enclosed. Include shipping and state taxes.

Please charge my: Visa / MasterCard (circle one)

Card #: _____ Exp. date: _____

**Book Price: $11.95**

**Shipping:**   $3.00 for the first book and $1.00 for each additional book to cover shipping and handling within US, Canada, and Mexico. International orders add $6.00 for the first book and $2.00 for each additional book.

### Or order from:
### ACW Press • 85334 Lorane Hwy • Eugene, OR  97405
### (800) 931-BOOK

### Or contact your local bookstore